SEEDS OF HEAVEN

Morehouse Publishing
P.O. Box 1321
Harrisburg, PA 17105

Morehouse Publishing is a division of The Morehouse Group.

Printed in Malaysia
Jacket design by Trude Brummer

05 04 03 02 01 00   5 4 3 2

Library of Congress Cataloging-in-Publication Data

Henry, Kim, 1961–
    Seeds of Heaven / written by Kim M. Henry; illustrated by
Mary Anne Lard.
        p.   cm.
    Summary: As a boy and his father walk from their home to the
seashore, they witness the wonders of all God has made. Includes
selected Bible verses.
    ISBN 0-8192-1791-3 (hardcover)
    1. Nature—Religious aspects—Christianity Juvenile literature.
    2. Creation Juvenile literature. 3. Jesus Christ—Parables
    Juvenile I. Lard, Mary Anne, ill. II. Title.
BT695.5.H465   1999
242—dc21   99-20292
                                                                CIP

Seeds of Heaven

Written by Kim M. Henry
Illustrated by Mary Anne Lard

MOREHOUSE PUBLISHING

A boy and his father took a late afternoon walk through the woods, to the place where the trees parted and the land rolled down to the sea. The sky was brilliant blue when they reached the clearing and looked over the hillside. "Can we see heaven from here?" asked the boy.

"Not exactly," said his father. "But we can see the farmers' fields and the salt water marsh that lies beyond. We can see white sand dunes and an azure sea."

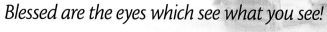

Blessed are the eyes which see what you see!

Luke 10:23

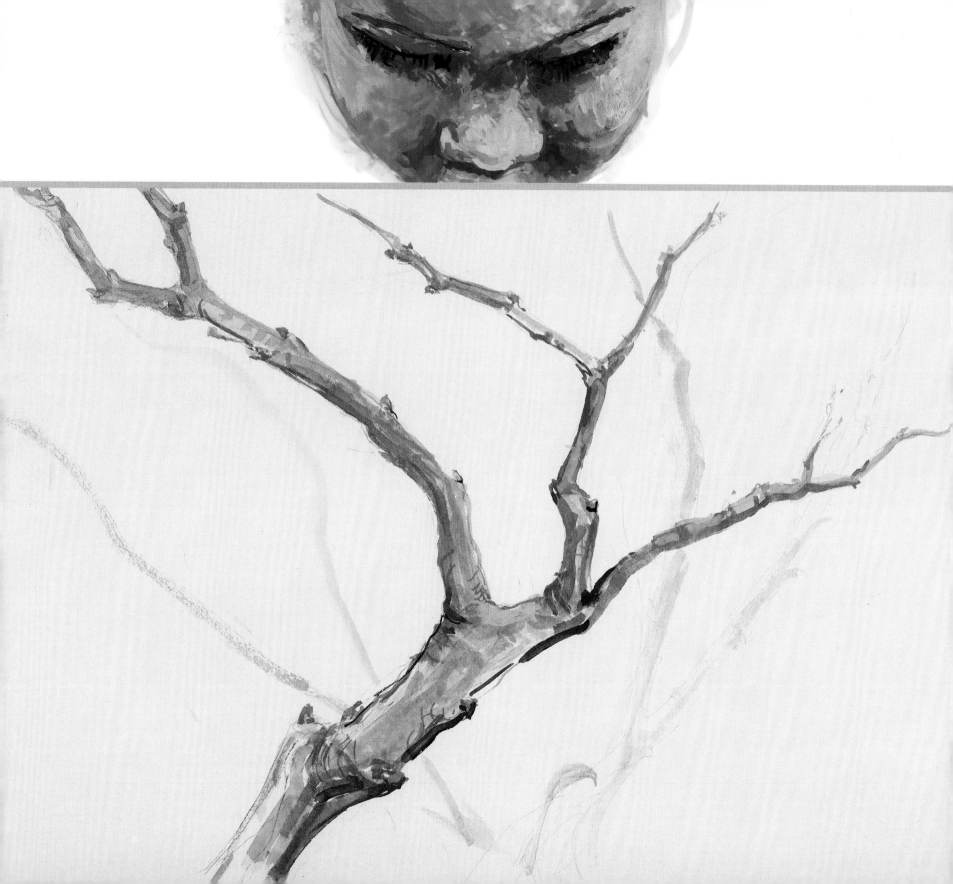

"On a spring day, we can see tiny buds on the branches of trees. And the next day we can see that the buds have opened into tender green leaves."

Look at the fig tree, and all the trees; as soon as they come out in leaf, you see for yourselves and know that the summer is already near.

Luke 21:29–30

"Have you noticed that after we plant our garden with packets of seeds, the soil seems brown and bare for many days? But when we look closely, we can see the smallest of sprouts. We can see a line of green speckles in the rows where we planted our seeds."

The kingdom of God is as if a man should scatter seed upon the ground, and should sleep and rise night and day, and the seed should sprout and grow, he knows not how.

Mark 4:26–27

The boy and his father walked on the gravel road that stretched from the farmland to the sea. Lilies bright as sunshine crowded the edge of the road and danced in the breeze. "Who planted this garden?" the boy asked.

"The wild flowers grow without our help," said the father, "but they are dressed as splendidly as kings."

*Consider the lilies of the
field, how they grow;
they neither toil nor spin;
yet I tell you, even Solomon
in all his glory was not
arrayed like one of these.*

Matthew 6:28–29

At the edge of the farmer's field, something was hidden in the brush. "Look!" said the father. "A meadowlark's nest!"

The speckled eggs sat like jewels in a crown. The boy had never seen a nest so well hidden. "It's just as safe as in a tree!" he said, pointing to the top of a large oak tree.

The kingdom of heaven is like treasure hidden in a field…

Matthew 13:44

The oak tree was covered with sparrows
that shook its branches. "Can you imagine
that such a big tree was once a small acorn
like this?" asked the father.

"Really?" said the boy, and he put the acorn
in his pocket.

The kingdom of heaven is like a grain of mustard seed which a man took and sowed in his field; it is the smallest of all seeds, but when it has grown it is the greatest of shrubs and becomes a tree, so that the birds of the air come and make nests in its branches.

Matthew 13:31–32

When the boy
and his father
reached the seashore,
they heard the sound
of waves rushing
on the sand.
The water lapped
at their toes
and the ocean air
left a salty taste
on their lips.

Seagulls,
wheeling
above their heads,
called and laughed
in the wind.
Sandpipers
twittered
and chattered
on the wet sand.

He who has ears to hear, let him hear.

Matthew 13:9

The boy threw crusts
of bread to the gulls.
"Who will feed the birds
when I've gone home?"
he asked.

"The gulls are clever
fishermen," said the
father. "They snatch up
fish from the waves as
easily as bread crusts."

Look at the birds of the air:
they neither sow nor reap
nor gather into barns, and
yet your heavenly Father
feeds them.

Matthew 6:26

As the sun began to set, the tide
went out, leaving a pool of water
between the rocks. The warm,
shallow water was full of life.
The boy saw silver-colored
minnows and thin-legged crabs.
He held a starfish in his hands,
but the sea anemone looked like
a flower too delicate to pick.

The kingdom of heaven is like a net
which was thrown into the sea and
gathered fish of every kind.

Matthew 13:47

The boy rubbed his finger on the inside of an empty shell. The half shell was smooth and pearly white. "Can I make a pearl for Mama with this?" he asked.

"No, but oysters can," said the father. "An oyster living in a shell like this can turn a grain of sand into a lovely round pearl."

"Really?" said the boy, and he put the shell in his pocket.

The kingdom of heaven
is like a merchant in search
of fine pearls, who, on
finding one pearl of great
value, went and sold all
that he had and bought it.

Matthew 13:45–46

The boy and his father stayed at the beach until the sun dropped from sight. As they walked home, the stars came out in the indigo sky. The moon rose over the sand dunes and cast a silvery light on the gravel road.

"Look! We can see even in the dark," said the boy.

"Yes, we can," said the father. "The light from the stars, and the moon, and all the heavens will show us the way home."

I am the light of the world; he who follows me will not walk in darkness, but will have the light of life.

John 8:12

The leaves of the trees whispered in the evening breeze. "Hush, hush," they seemed to say, making the boy grow sleepy. The father swung the boy onto his shoulders and carried him the rest of the way. The boy was nearly asleep when he saw the light from the house glowing through the trees.

*Let the children come to me, and
do not hinder them; for to such
belongs the kingdom of God.*

Luke 18:16

When he got inside, the
boy told his mother about
all the beautiful things he
had seen. He showed her
the acorn and the shell.
"See, Mama," he said.
"I've brought you some
heaven in my pocket."

*To you it has been given to know the secrets
of the kingdom of heaven…*

Matthew 13:11

I THANK YOU, GOD, FOR ALL THESE THINGS,

THE BEAUTY THAT YOUR GOODNESS BRINGS:

A GRAIN OF SAND UPON THE BEACH,

 A BIRD THAT SOARS BEYOND MY REACH.

A STAR THAT SHINES AGAINST THE NIGHT,

A SINGLE RAY OF HEAVEN'S LIGHT.

A BUD THAT BLOSSOMS ON A TREE,

 A MIRACLE FOR ME TO SEE.

A SEED SO SMALL INSIDE MY HAND

BECOMES A TREE TO SHADE THE LAND.

I THANK YOU, GOD, FOR ALL THESE THINGS,

THE WONDER YOUR CREATION BRINGS.

ABOUT THE AUTHOR:

Kim Henry has been writing children's
books for ten years, as well as working
in the environmental field. Kim lives
with her husband and two children
in Groton, Massachusetts.

ABOUT THE ILLUSTRATOR:

Mary Anne Lard is a freelance
illustrator and artist and lives in
Carlisle, Pennsylvania. She is also
the illustrator of *Jenny's Prayer*.